James Whitbourn

LUMINOSITY

for SATB choir, viola, tanpura, tam-tam
and dance theatre

CHESTER MUSIC

Luminosity is a multi-media work, commissioned by the conductor James Jordan of Westminster Choir College for the Westminster Williamson Voices, the women of the Westminster *Schola Cantorum*, the Blair Academy Singers (conductor, William Hammer) and the black-light dance company *Archedream*, for performance in Philadelphia Cathedral during April 2008.

The text, compiled and edited by the composer, centres on the transcendent beauty of creation expressed by luminaries down the ages. Texts are taken from the writings of St John, St Teresa of Avila, Ryonen, St Augustine, Julian of Norwich, and St Isaac of Nineveh.

Scoring

SATB (with divisions)
viola
tanpura
tam-tam
organ

Duration

c. 30 minutes

Cover illustration by Robert Tear C.B.E.

Performance materials are available on sale:
full/chorus score: CH73502
set of parts (viola, tanpura, tam-tam): CH73502-01

A recording of *Luminosity* is available on the Naxos label
Naxos CD: 8.572103

Composer's Note:

Luminosity is divided into seven sections which merge together to create a continuous piece. Although there are short silences within the piece, the music should never stop or pause until its end.

The work is conceived with a visual counterpoint to the music in mind, coming in the form of art, dance and light as well as in the use of space. The focus in all the elements is on transcendent beauty and eternal love. It is likely to be symbolic, luminous and shapely in concept.

Ideally the violist will have some understanding of Karnatic performance style and will incorporate appropriate stylistic detail into the score from time to time, especially when the writing is at its most improvisational.

The drone is an important element in the work, led by the tanpura, with its distinctive and timeless quality of sound. Ideally the tanpura will be placed at some distance from the main body of choral voices. Voices and organ also form part of the drone at different times. A four-stringed tanpura should be tuned to the pitches D – A – D – D. No other pitches should be used.
It is recommended that an instrument with a suitably long neck is found which can produce a resonant low D. On no account should the instrument be electronically amplified.
At the start of movements I, IV and VI, the tanpura should repeat several times the pattern of notes shown, to build resonance and establish the drone before the movement continues.

I am grateful to my friend Robert Tear, not only for his beautiful illustration drawn to adorn this piece, but also for introducing me to several of the texts in our many conversations on the Spirit.

JW

LIBRETTO

I. Lux in tenebris
Illuminare

Lux in tenebris lucet et tenebrae eam non comprehenderunt.
(The light shines in darkness and the darkness has not overpowered it.)

John the Apostle (*c*.6 – *c*.100)

II. The Changing Scenes
Sixty-six times have these eyes beheld the changing scenes of autumn.
I have said enough about moonlight,
ask me no more.
Only listen to the voice of cedars and pines,
when no wind stirs.

Ryonen, Zen Buddhist nun (b. 1797)

III. Silence
Silence is a mystery of the age to come,
but words are instruments of this world.

Isaac of Nineveh (d. *c*.700)

Lux in tenebris lucet.

IV. The Living Thing
He showed me a little thing,
the size of a hazelnut,
in the palm of my hand,
I looked at it with my mind's eye and thought, 'What can this be?'
And answer came, 'It is all that is made.'
I marvelled that it could last.
And answer came into my mind,
'It lasts and ever shall because God loves it.'
And all things have being through the love of God.

Julian of Norwich (1342 – *c*.1416)

V. Castle of Diamonds   page 54

It came to me that the soul is like a castle,
a castle of diamond or other clear crystal.
In this castle are a multitude of dwellings,
just as in heaven there are many mansions.

                                        Teresa of Avila (1515 – 1582)

VI. Ask the Beauty   page 58

Ask the beauty of the earth,
Ask the beauty of the sea,
Ask the beauty of the sky.
Question the order of the stars,
the sun whose brightness lights the day,
the moon whose splendour softens the gloom of Night.
Ask the living creatures that move in the waves,
Ask the living creatures that roam the earth,
Ask the living creatures that fly in the heavens.
Question them and they will answer,
"Yes, we are beautiful."
Their very loveliness is their confession to God:
for who made these lovely mutable things,
but he who himself is unchangeable beauty?

                                        Augustine of Hippo (354-430)

VII. All Shall be Well   page 74

Because of our good Lord's tender love to all who shall be saved,
he quickly comforts them, saying,
"The cause of all this pain is sin.
But all shall be well, and all shall be well,
and all manner of things shall be well."

                                        Julian of Norwich

Alleluia.

LUMINOSITY

JAMES WHITBOURN

I. Lux in tenebris

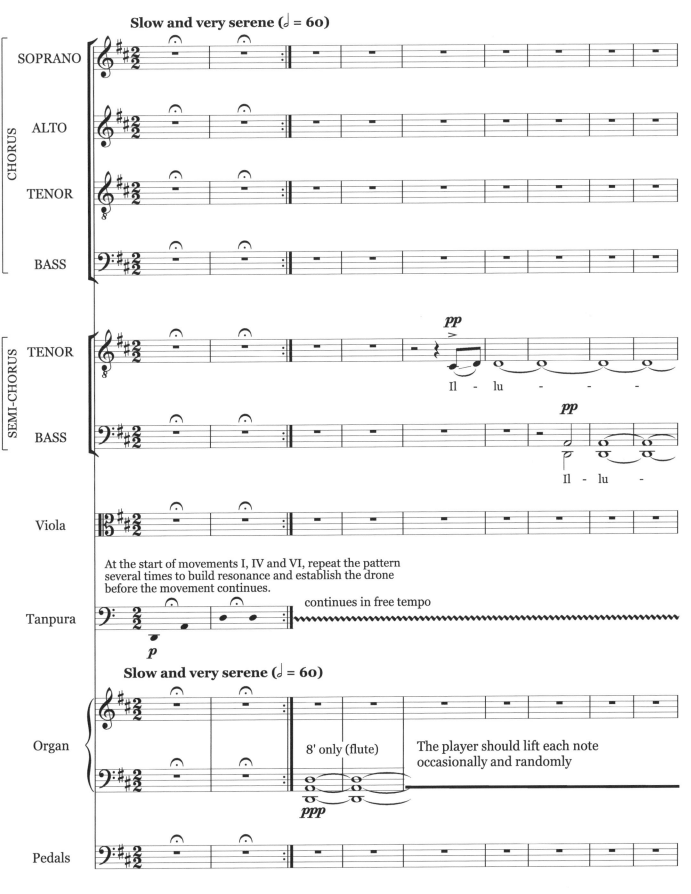

At the start of movements I, IV and VI, repeat the pattern several times to build resonance and establish the drone before the movement continues.

continues in free tempo

8' only (flute)

The player should lift each note occasionally and randomly

rev. 16/06/2011

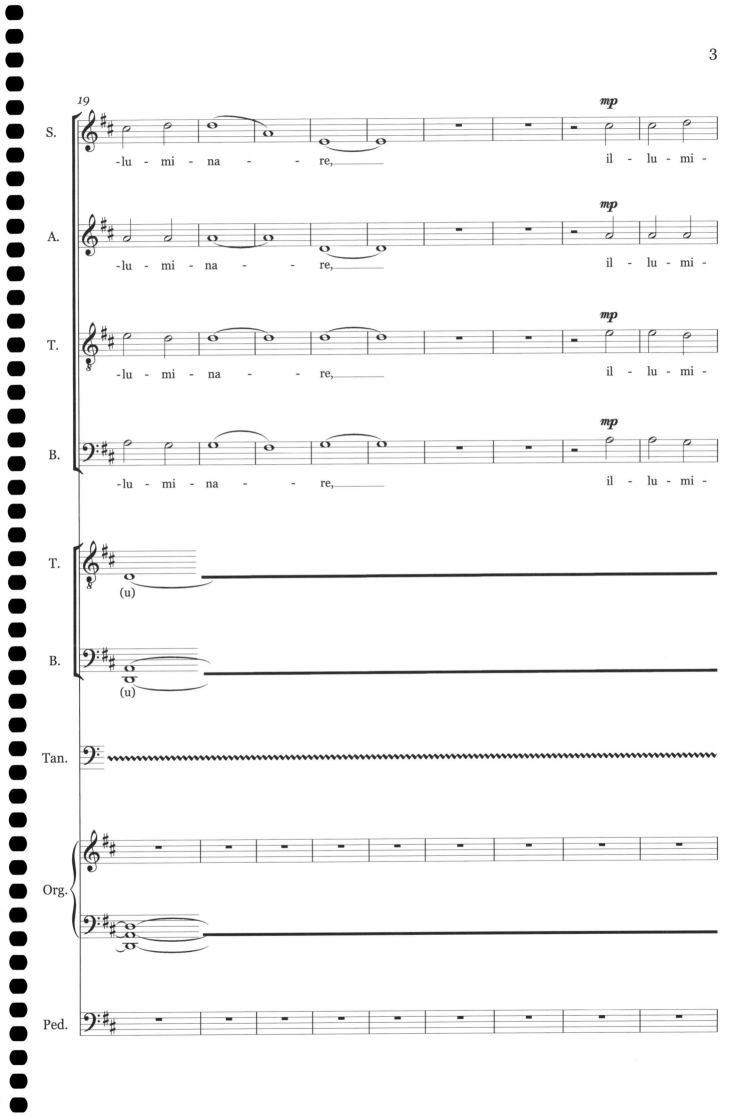

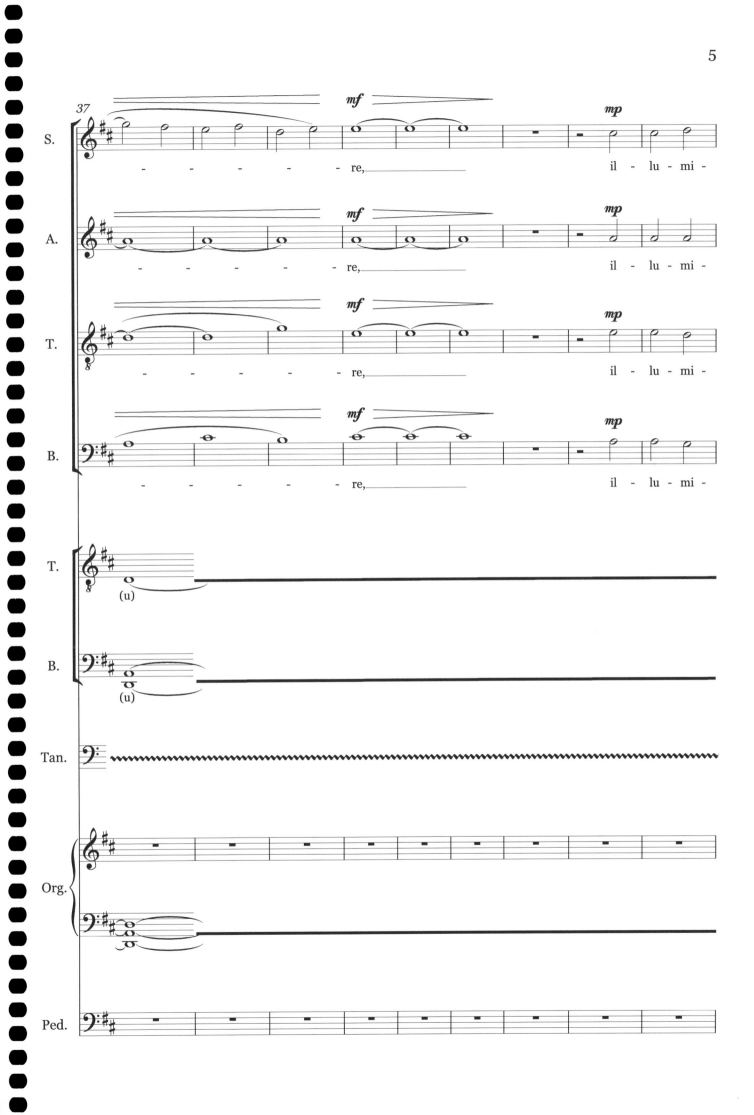

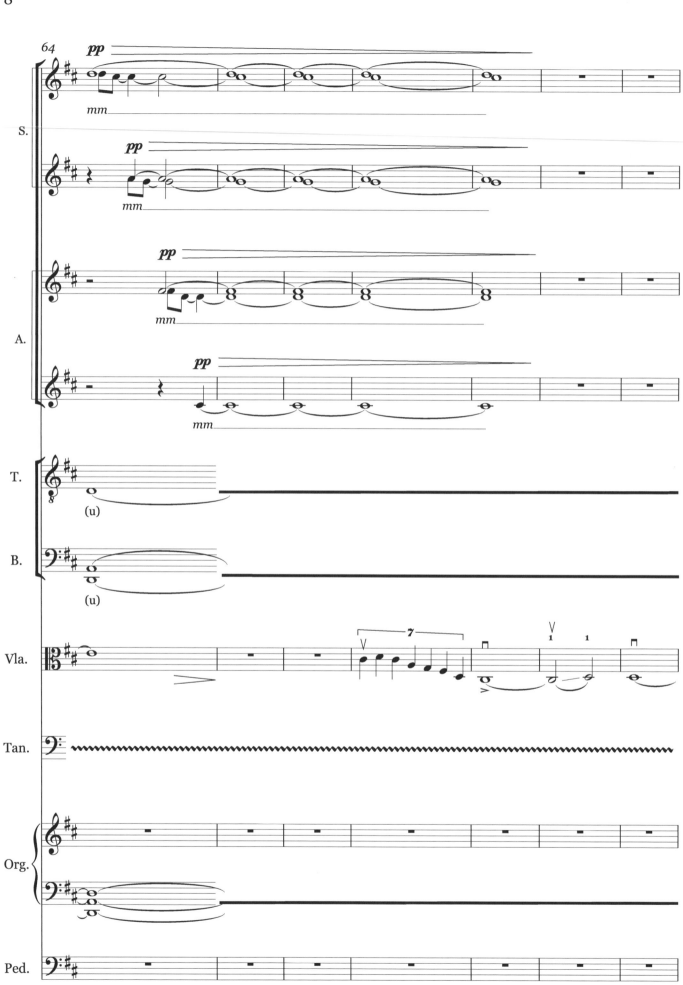

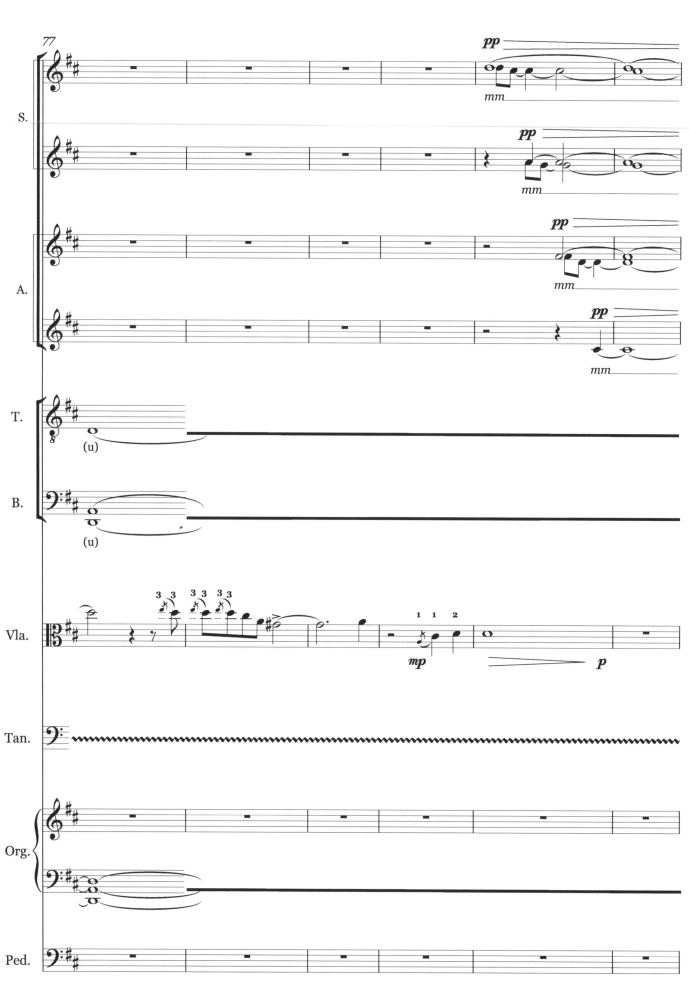

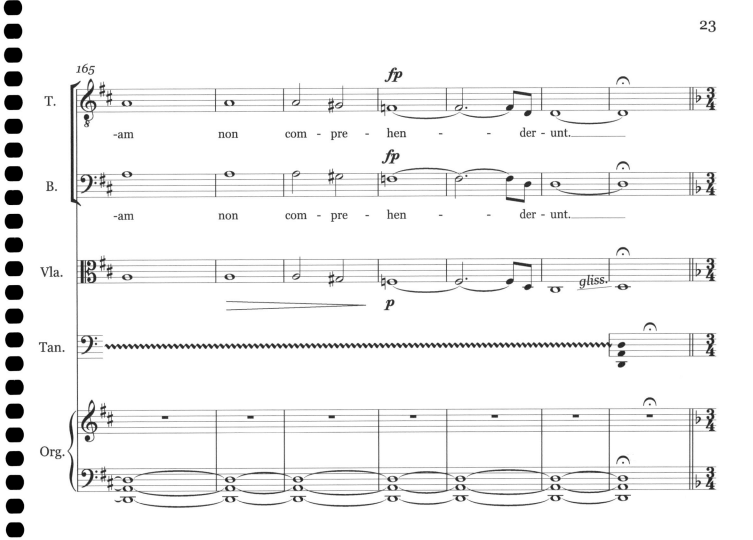

II. The Changing Scenes

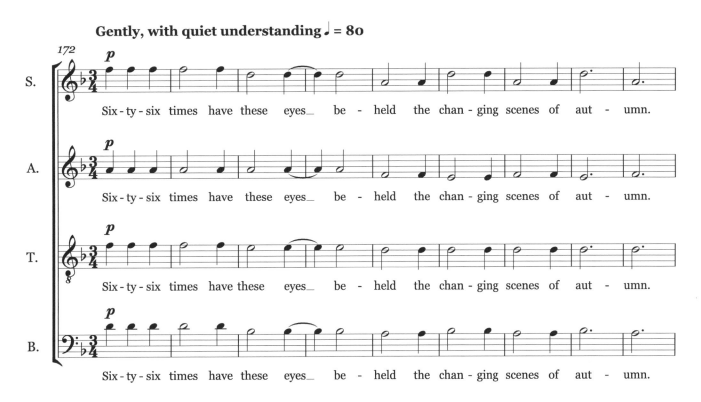

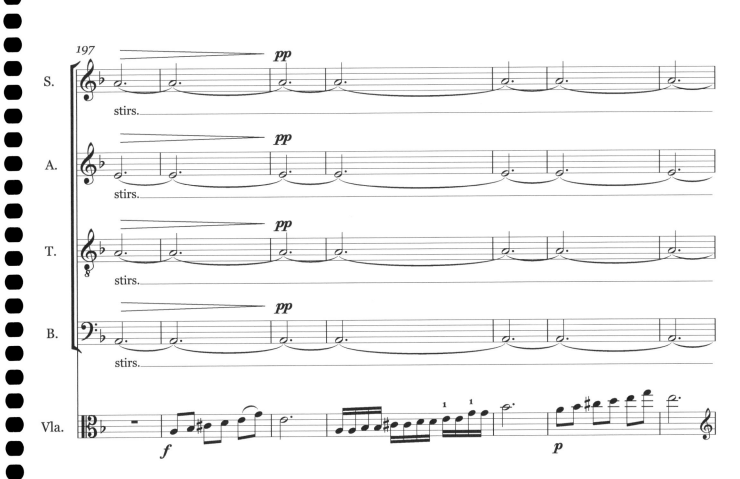

III. Silence

With mystery and awe ♩ = 54

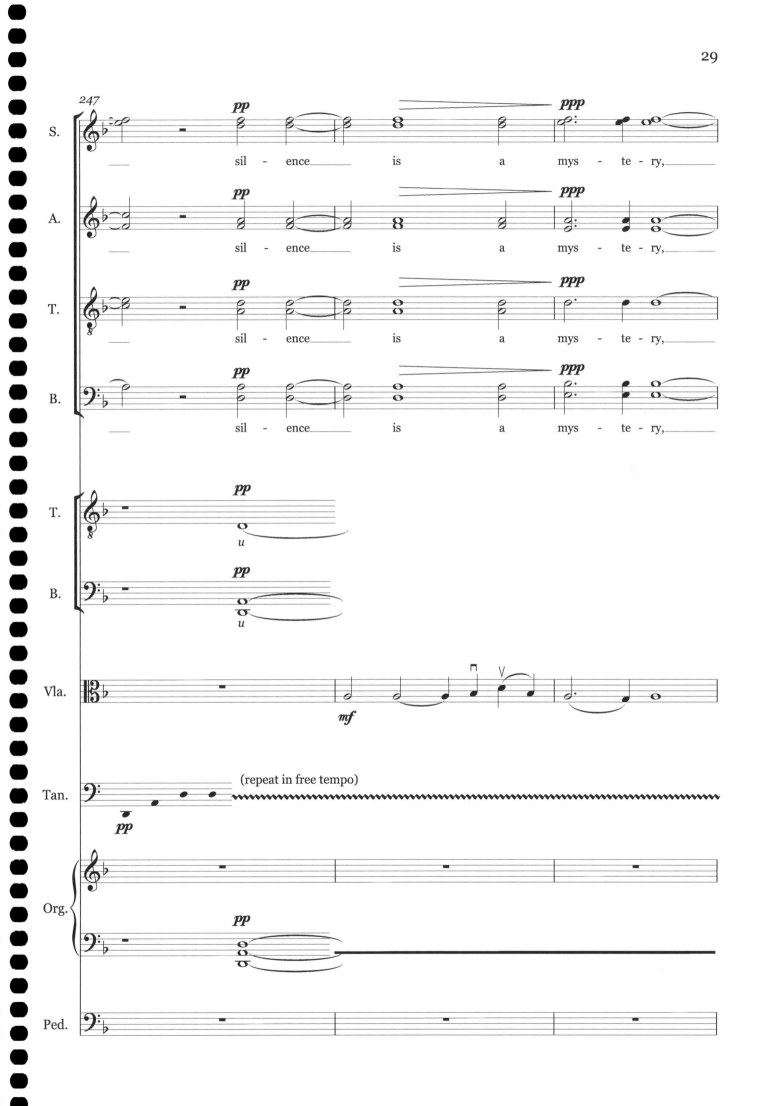

36

IV. The Living Thing

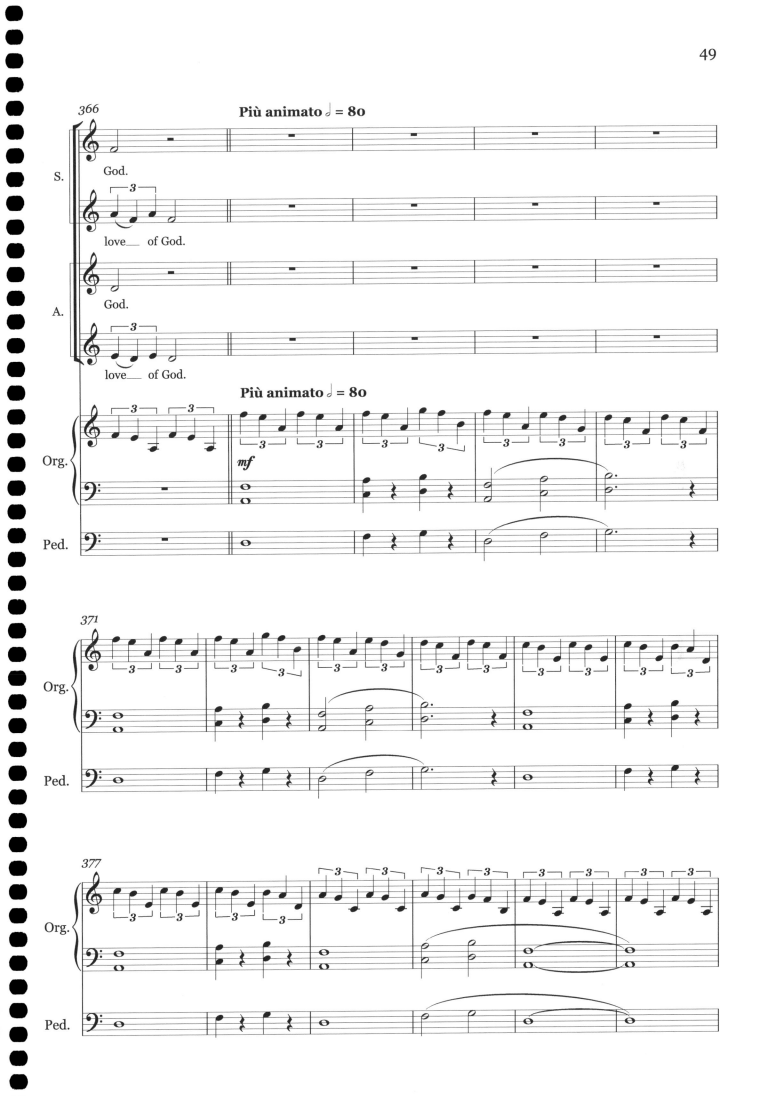

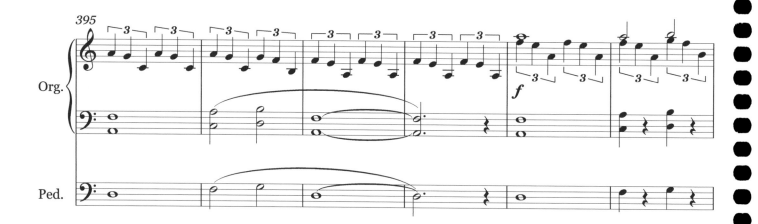

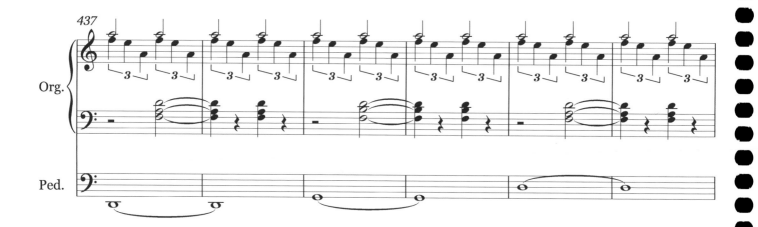

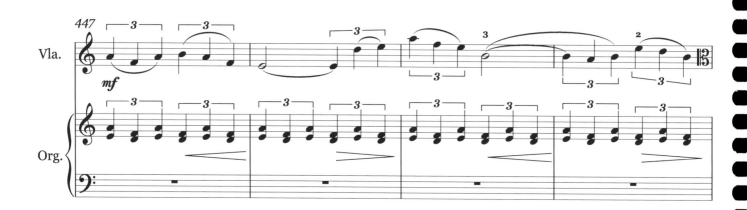

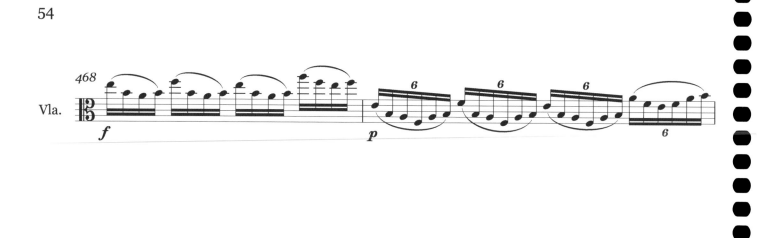

V. Castle of Diamonds

* sounds *uh*

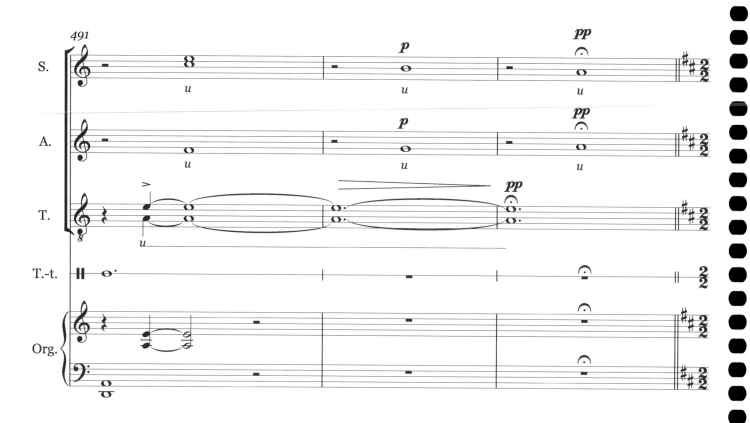

VI. Ask the Beauty

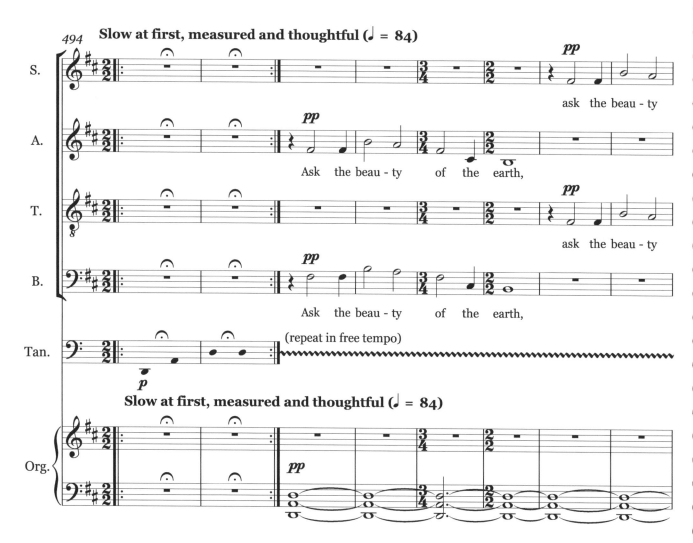

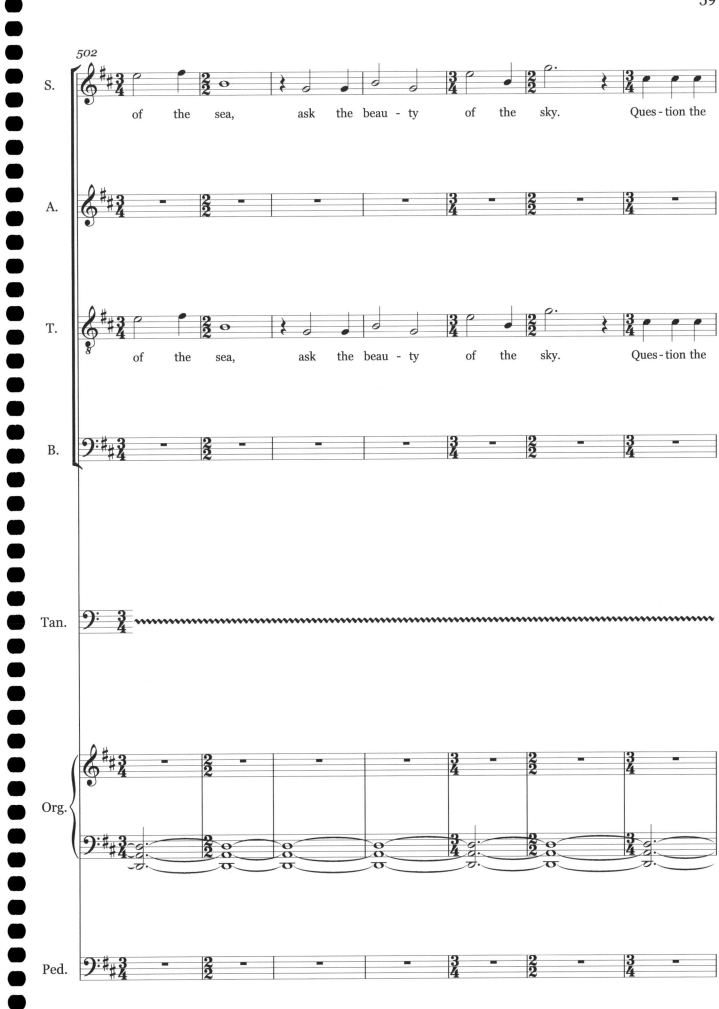

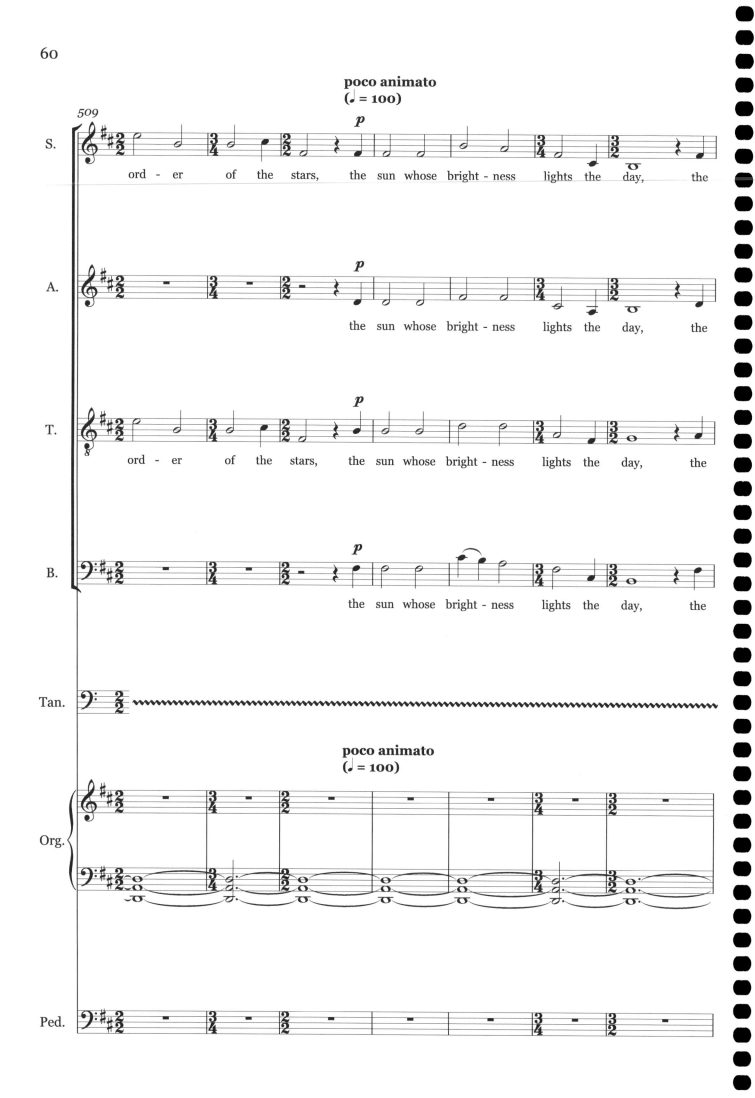

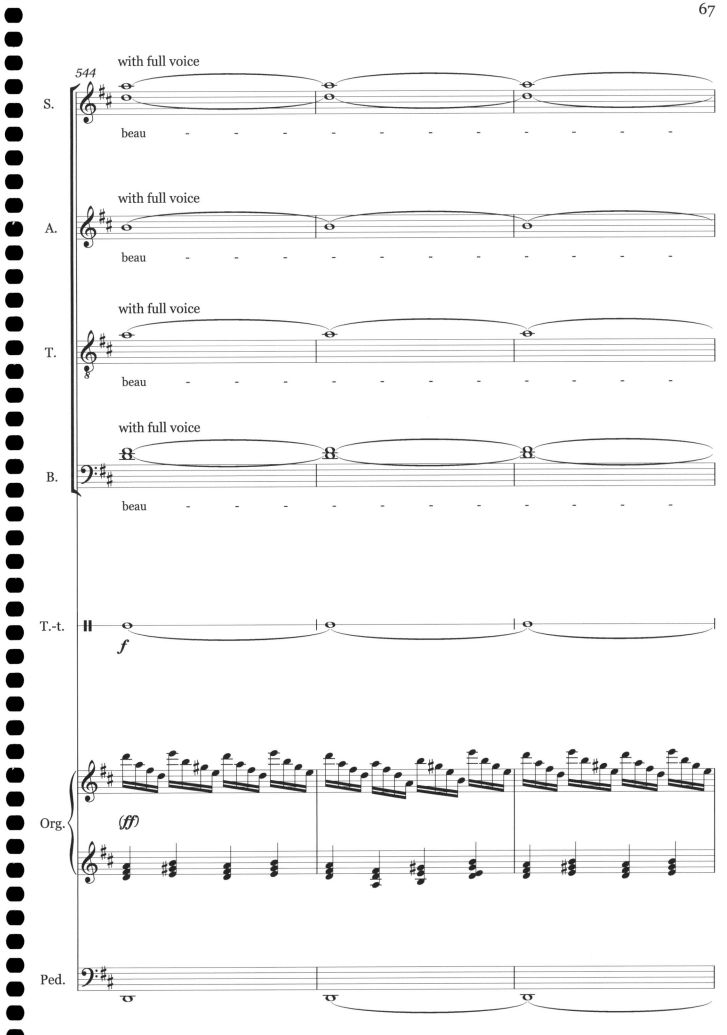

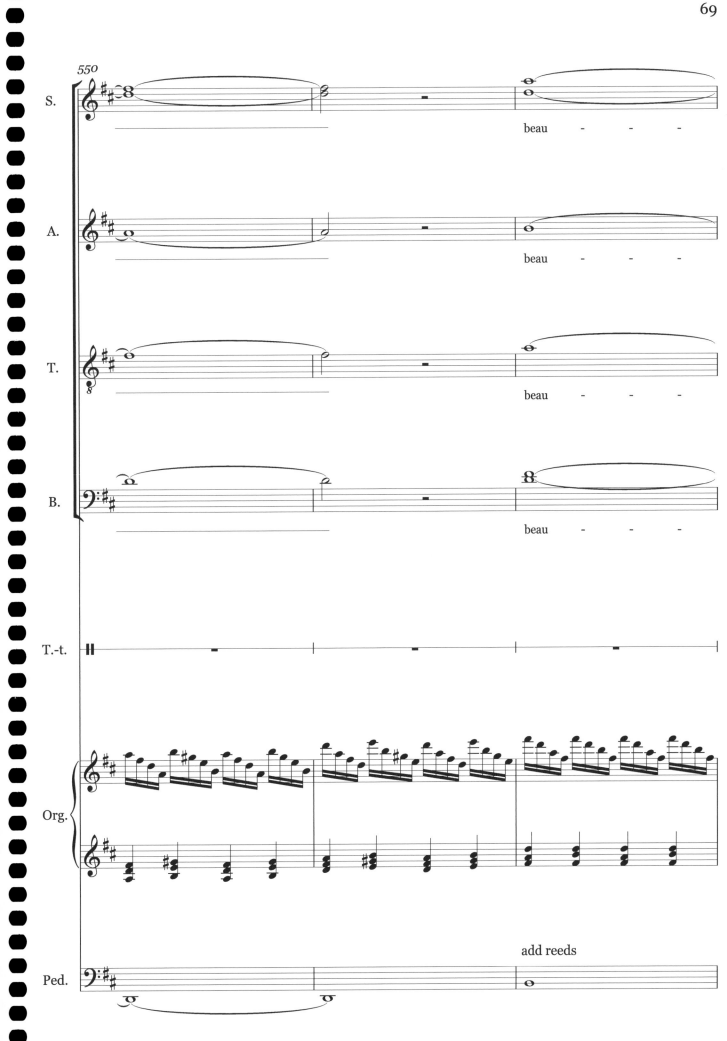

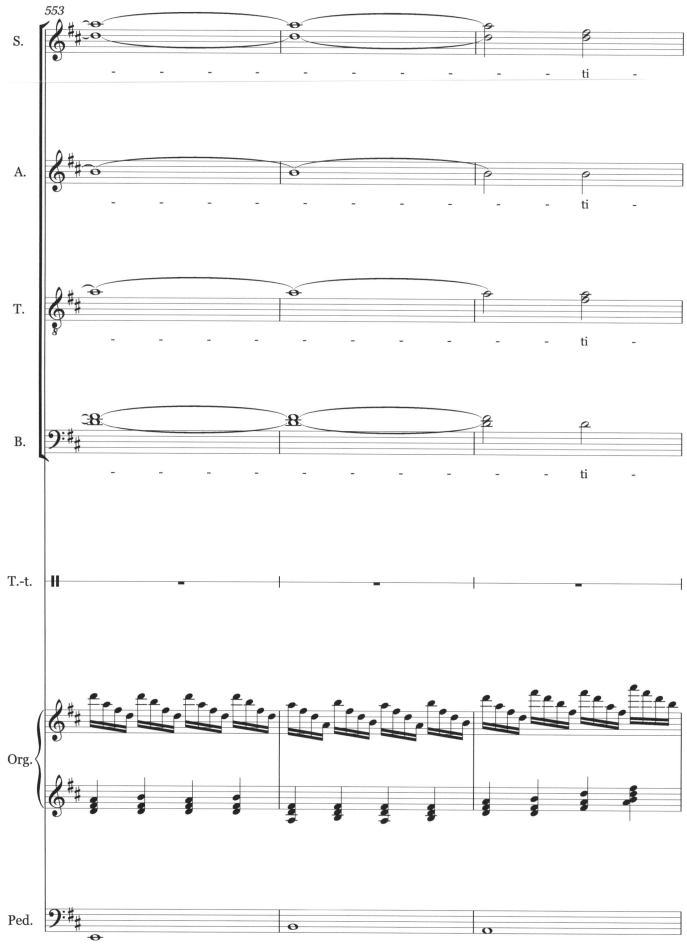

* sounds *uh*

VII. All Shall be Well

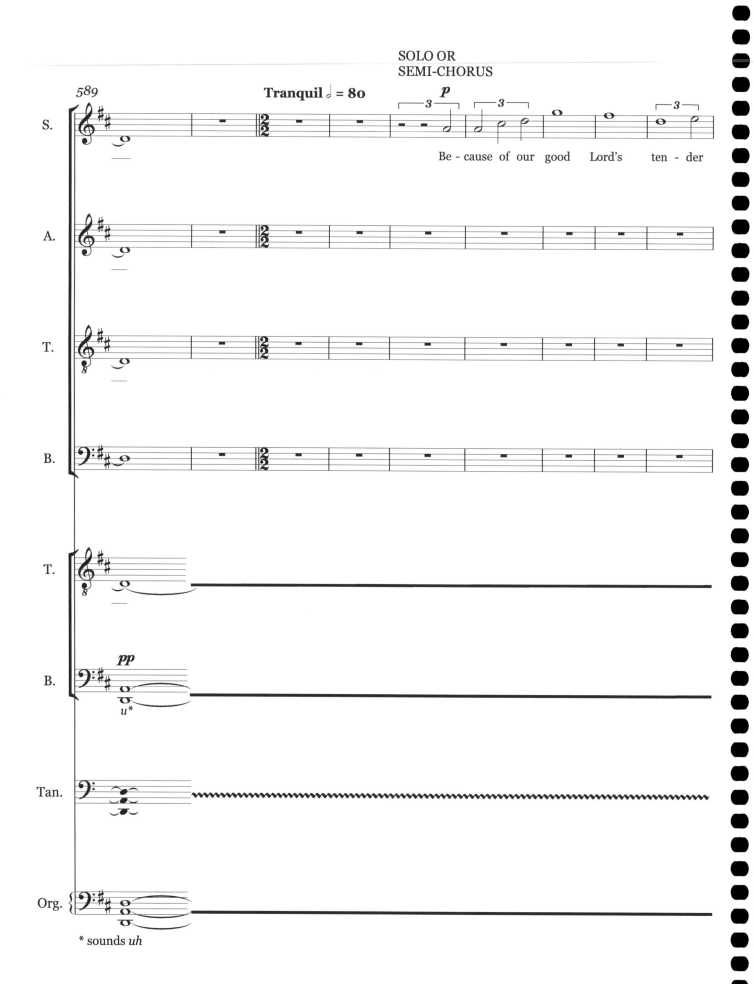

* sounds *uh*

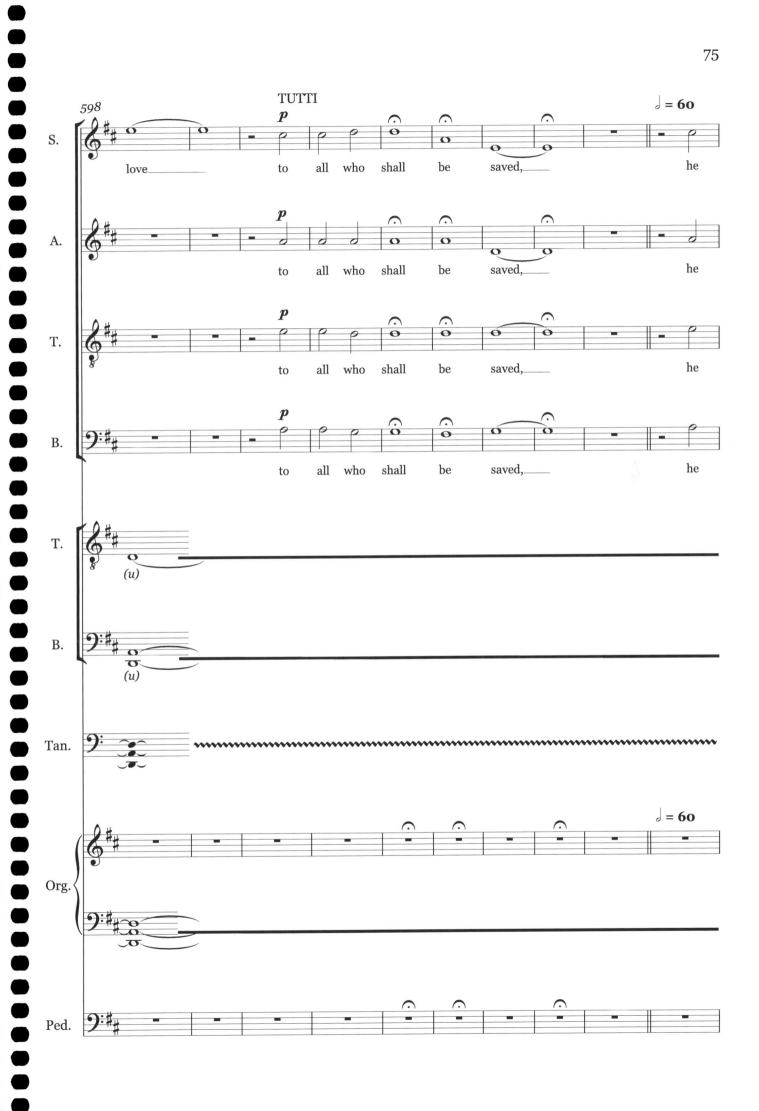

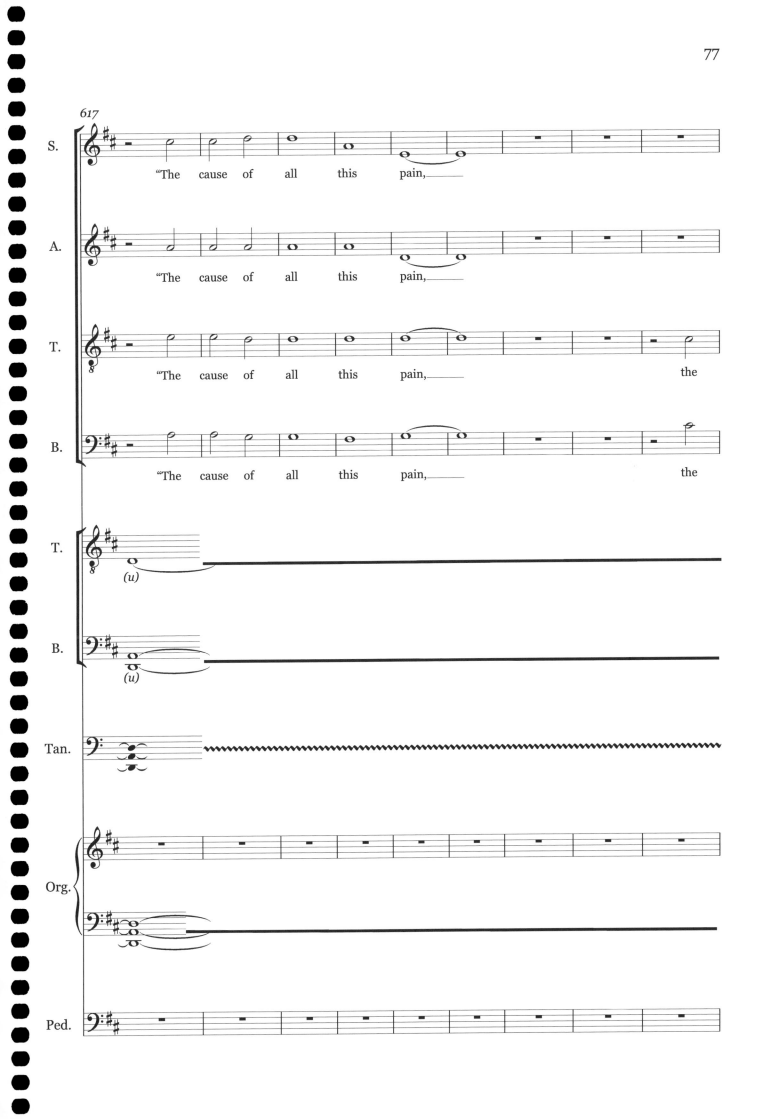

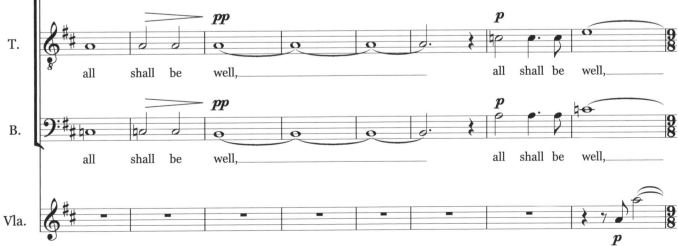

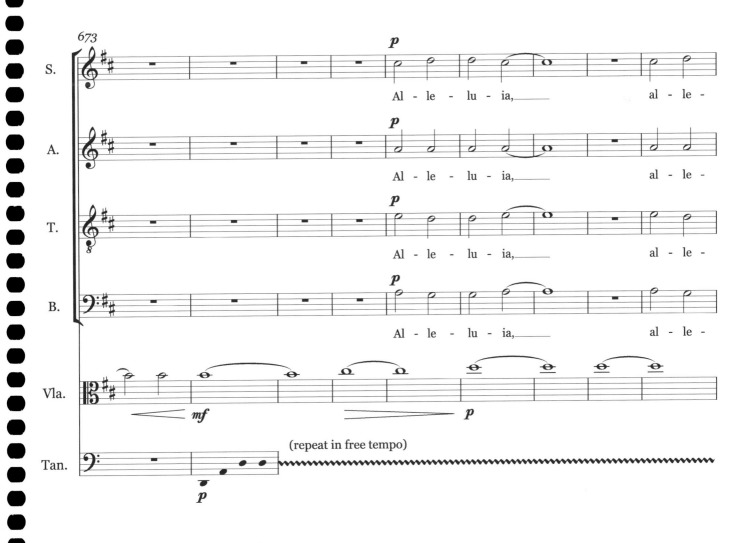

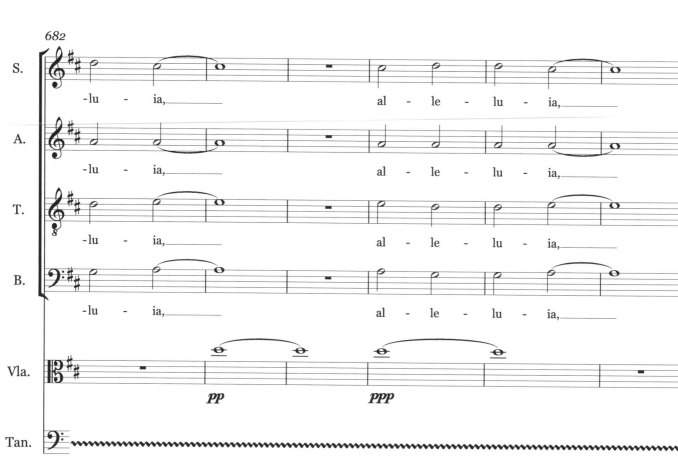

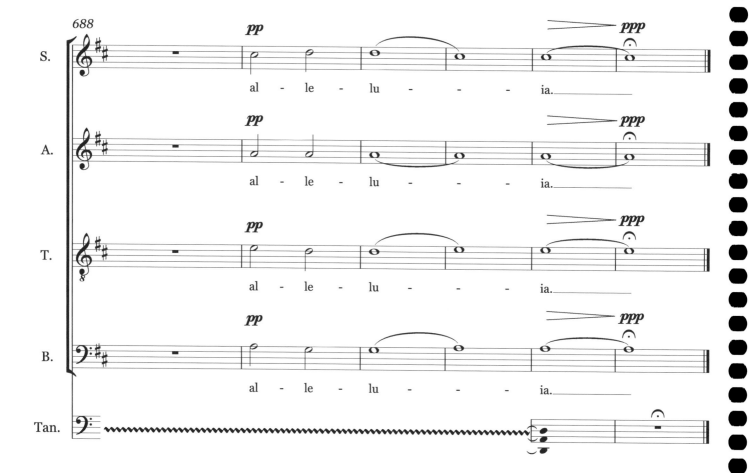

CHESTER MUSIC

part of **WiseMusic**Group

EXCLUSIVELY DISTRIBUTED BY
HAL•LEONARD®

Exclusive distributors
Hal Leonard Europe Limited
1 Red Place
London, W1K 6PL
www.halleonard.com

MUSCH73502

5 020679 262986 >